LIVES
AND
TIMES

Queen Elizabeth 1

Rachael Bell

Heinemann
LIBRARY

First published in Great Britain by Heinemann Library
Halley Court, Jordan Hill, Oxford OX2 8EJ,
a division of Reed Educational and Professional Publishing Ltd.
Heinemann is a registered trademark of Reed Educational & Professional Publishing Limited.

OXFORD FLORENCE PRAGUE MADRID ATHENS
MELBOURNE AUCKLAND KUALA LUMPUR SINGAPORE TOKYO
IBADAN NAIROBI KAMPALA JOHANNESBURG GABORONE
PORTSMOUTH NH (USA) CHICAGO MEXICO CITY SAO PAULO

Designed by Ken Vail Graphic Design, Cambridge
Illustrations by Sean Victory
Printed in Hong Kong / China

02 01 00 99 98
10 9 8 7 6 5 4 3 2 1

ISBN 0 431 02498 7

British Library Cataloguing in Publication Data

Bell, Rachael
Queen Elizabeth I. - (Lives & times)
1. Elizabeth, I, Queen of England, 1533–1603 - Juvenile literature
2. Queens - England - Biography - Juvenile literature 3. Great Britain - History - Elizabeth I, 1558–1603 - Juvenile literature
I. Title
942' .055'092

Some words are shown in bold, **like this**. You can find out what they mean by looking in the glossary. The glossary also helps you say difficult words.

Acknowledgements

The Publishers would like to thank the following for permission to reproduce photographs:

Mansell Collection p19; National Maritime Museum p20; National Portrait Gallery pp16, 17; National Trust p22; Shakespeare's Globe p23; Staatliche Museen, Kassel p18; Victoria and Albert Museum p21

Cover photograph reproduced with permission of Bridgeman Art Library

Our thanks to Betty Root for her comments in the preparation of this book.

Every effort has been made to contact copyright holders of any material reproduced in this book. Any omissions will be rectified in subsequent printings if notice is given to the Publisher.

Contents

The first part of this book tells you the story of Elizabeth I.
The second part tells you how you can find out about her life.

Childhood

Princess Elizabeth was born on 7th September 1533. Her father, King Henry VIII, married six times altogether. Her mother was his second wife.

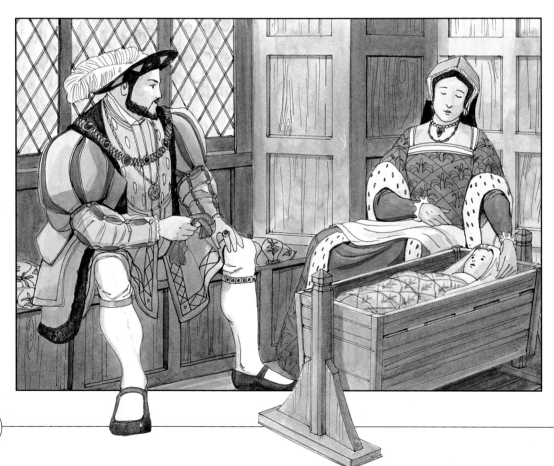

When Elizabeth was only three years old
her father had her mother **executed**.
Elizabeth had no proper family or home.
She must have been lonely and sad.

Growing up

Henry's sixth wife arranged for Elizabeth to be educated. She had the best private teachers and learnt many languages. She also learned to ride and enjoy music.

Henry VIII had tried to stamp out the **Catholic** Church. Later, Elizabeth's older sister, Mary, became queen. She wanted everyone to be a Catholic. She was cruel to the **Protestants**.

Queen of England

Most people were very glad when Mary I died. They hoped that all the **religious** hatred and cruelty would stop. Elizabeth was 25 when she was crowned Queen Elizabeth I.

Elizabeth was very wise. She chose good advisers. She knew she had to keep both the **Catholics** and the **Protestants** happy. Elizabeth was good at not taking sides.

Troubles

Elizabeth faced many dangers. When she was 29 she almost died of **smallpox**. Her advisers begged her to marry and have a child. They wanted her to have an **heir**.

Some **Catholics** in England, and others from France and Spain, wanted to get rid of Elizabeth. They wanted her Catholic cousin, Mary Queen of Scots, to rule England.

Help

Elizabeth was supported by her sailors. They brought her back riches, from buying and selling overseas. They also raided other ships, especially Spanish ones!

The Spanish king sent his **Armada** to
invade England in 1588. He had heard that
Mary Queen of Scots had been **beheaded**.
Elizabeth's sailors defeated them.

Popular

Elizabeth died in 1603, aged 69.

She had always been a strong queen.

'Good Queen Bess' was liked in
England and famous in other countries.

Elizabeth did so much. She brought peace to England and made the church right for most people. The country became richer because of the success of her sailors.

Paintings

Elizabeth was the king's daughter, so she was important enough to be painted. This painting shows us what she looked like when she was 13 years old.

When she was queen, Elizabeth stopped people from painting her unless she gave them special permission. She made sure that she always looked beautiful and powerful.

Paintings

This painting shows how people lived in Elizabeth's palace. Two Dutch visitors are kneeling in front of Elizabeth. No one else has a chair. They have to stand or sit on the floor.

Books

Books can tell us about the **religious** troubles. The *Foxe's Book of **Martyrs*** was printed in Elizabeth's time. It shows how many **Protestants** were cruelly killed by Mary I.

Artefacts

Elizabeth always believed that God was on her side and that he had sent a storm to destroy the Spanish **Armada**. She had a special medal made. It says 'God breathed and they were scattered' in Latin.

We also know that Elizabeth studied music. You can still see her keyboard or 'virginals' which she played as a young princess.

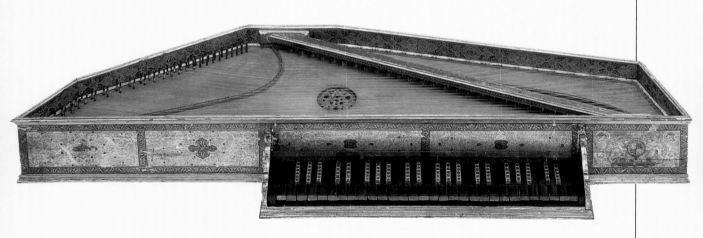

Buildings

Elizabeth brought peace and wealth to England. Many beautiful houses were built in her time. Penshurst Place in Kent is one of them.

The Globe theatre was first built in 1599.
Shakespeare's new plays were
performed there. Now, The Globe has
been rebuilt. Queen Elizabeth II saw one of
Shakespeare's plays there in 1997.

Glossary

Armada Spanish war ships. You say *ar-mar-da*

artefacts things which survive from the past that tell us more about it

beheaded put to death by chopping off the head

Catholic Christians who have the Pope in Rome as the head of their church – the Roman Catholic Church

executed put to death as a punishment for a crime

heir someone to be the next ruler when she died. You say *air*

martyr someone who is killed for their beliefs. You say *mar-tur*

performed acted out in front of an audience

Protestant Christians who do not have the Pope as the head of the church – they broke away from the Roman Catholic Church in the 1500s

religious to do with people's belief or religion

Shakespeare's written by William Shakespeare – he wrote many famous plays in Queen Elizabeth I's reign and after

smallpox a disease which was caught very easily and killed many people – sufferers had blisters and spots

Index